The Human Slaughter-House

Scenes From The War That Is Sure To Come

by

Wilhelm Lamszus

Double 9 BOOKS

The Human Slaughter-House
Scenes From The War That Is Sure To Come
by Wilhelm Lamszus

ISBN: 978-93-62762-48-1

Published by

DOUBLE 9 BOOKS
2/13-B, Ansari Road
Daryaganj, New Delhi – 110002
info@double9books.com
www.double9books.com
Tel. 011-40042856

ABOUT THE AUTHOR

Wilhelm Lamszus, a prolific German author, penned the harrowing masterpiece "The Human Slaughter-House: Scenes from the War that is Sure to Come," a prophetic work that delves into the grim realities of war. Lamszus's novel offers a chilling glimpse into the horrors of modern warfare, foreseeing the devastation and brutality that would engulf the world in the coming years. Through vivid and haunting prose, Lamszus paints a stark portrait of the human cost of conflict, portraying the suffering, sacrifice, and loss experienced by soldiers and civilians alike. With meticulous attention to detail, he captures the chaos and carnage of battle, while also exploring the psychological toll of war on individuals and societies. "The Human Slaughter-House" stands as a powerful testament to Lamszus's foresight and his commitment to exposing the true nature of war. As a timeless work of literature, it serves as a solemn reminder of the need for peace and understanding in a world plagued by violence and strife.

CONTENTS

INTRODUCTION

*There is one thing that will certainly be said about this book by some of its readers. It will certainly be said to exaggerate the horrors of modern war; and, just as certainly, that is a thing which this book does not do. It is appallingly reticent; and, for every touch of horror in its pages, the actual records of recent warfare could supply an obscure and blood-stained mass of detail which, if it were once laid before the public, would put an end to militarism in a year. It is not the opponents of militarism who are given over to "cant" and "hypocrisy" and "emotionalism." It is the supporters of militarism who on the eve of a great war go about crying for suppression of facts, censorship of the facts not only of military plans, but of human suffering. For if there is one thing that the military journalist dreads it is the sight and smell of blood. "Let us enjoy this pleasant compaign. Let us present our readers with a little military music played upon the brass bands of the press. But for God's sake do not waft over Europe the smell of iodoform, or of the slaughter-house. Man is a fighting animal; let us enjoy the fight. And—*pollice verso!"

Unfortunately for these gentlemen, whose good taste is so impeccable that they shrink from the whole truth, man is also a fighting god. 'And the next thing we are going to fight is militarism. There is hardly a great commander in the history of modern warfare who has not described his own profession as "a dirty trade" and war itself as hell. The party of "bad taste" which is going to destroy militarism is not likely to reject the testimony of Wellington, Grant and Napier in favor of the sensational journalist. This book deals chiefly with the physical and mental horrors of war. It presents just that one side of the case; but it must not be forgotten that there are vast battalions of logic and common sense on the same side. From a logical point of view a war between civilized peoples is as insane as it is foul and evil. The pacificists are fighting the noblest battle of the present day. They are not going to win without a struggle; but they will win. And they will win because they have on their side the common good of mankind, common sense, common justice, and common truth.

ALFRED NOYES.

WILHELM LAMSZUS

Few books of its size—one hundred and eleven pages in the original edition—can perhaps of recent years claim the striking and instantaneous success of Wilhelm Lamszus's "Menschenschlachthaus." In appraising this success, I am less concerned with the number of copies sold (which now, three months after publication, approximates, I believe, one hundred thousand) than with the impression it has left on the mind of its readers in Germany and elsewhere on the Continent. Within a few days of its publication the author awoke to find himself famous—or infamous, according to the point of view adopted—in his own country. The fact that his book has been, or is being, translated into no less than eight European languages is evidence that its appeal is not confined to the conditions of one country, or of a single nationality.

Its appeal is broad-based. It is addressed to the conscience of civilized humanity, and as was to have been expected, the conscience of the individual has reacted to its stimulus in various ways.

The first evidence the author received of the success of his work was drastic. By profession he is a master at one of the great German public schools. He was at once "relieved" of his duties, but has now, I understand, been reinstated. The schoolmaster in Germany, it must be borne in mind, is primarily a state official. His most important function is to educate, not only the rising generation of citizens, but the future levies of conscripts. For a schoolmaster to write a book "with a tendency" to strip the pomp and circumstance of war of its traditional glamour—an integral factor in the German educational system—must, in the eyes of the orthodox of the "State-conserving" parties, have savored of an unholy alliance between blasphemy and high treason. The sale of the book was interdicted in the town of its first publication—the "free" city of Hamburg. The interdict had the effect of stimulating its sale elsewhere. It challenged a hearing. Even the "State-conserving" journals were unable to ignore it entirely.

A short time ago, in an open letter addressed to the German press, the author replied to the criticisms and strictures of his professional reviewers. As may be conceived, these criticisms and strictures lacked nothing in virulence or acrimony. "A peril to the public safety," "an hysterical neuropath," "a morbid phantasy," "a socialist-anarchic revolutionary," "a cowardly weakling," "a landless man," "an imported alien draining the marrow of patriotic backbone," may serve as an anthology (for which I am mainly indebted to the *Hamburger Nachrichten*) of the compliments showered on the author and his work. As this reply discloses what was in the author's mind when he wrote his book, definitely explains its purport and its purpose, it may be worth some consideration. It may serve to differentiate "The Human Slaughter-House" from the itch of mere literary sensationalism and enable the foreigner to understand the light in which the Commission for Instruction, Education, etc., of the nineteenth Universal Peace Congress at Geneva regarded it when last year it wrote officially to congratulate its author on having placed "a weapon of the greatest importance" in the hands of the pacificists.

At all times and at all places, Lamszus points out, patriotism has been of two kinds. The one sort takes its stand on the public market-place, with its hand on its manly chest, to advertise the public spirit that inflates it. In season and out of season, it never fails to invite the public gaze to dwell on the integrity of its patriotic sentiments. Its main strength lies in the spectacular and oratorical. As such it not infrequently deteriorates into the idle sound and fury of Junkerdom, Chauvinism and Jingoism.

There is that other type of patriotism that, no less loyal to its own country, believes in the dignity and worth of humanity, that believes in the patriotism of quiet, unadvertised, productive work and in the virtue of a sense of moral responsibility. It is sanguine enough to believe that it may yet be the destiny of a great nation to serve the cause of humanity by eliminating the hideous necessity for war. It finds its highest representative in the patriot of the type of the late Emperor Frederick the Noble, who, himself a soldier proven on the stricken field, found the courage to say, "I hate the business of blood. You have never seen war. If you had ever seen it you would not speak the word unmoved. I have seen it, and I tell you it is a man's highest duty to avoid war if by any means it can be avoided."

The issue Lamszus raises at the bar of public opinion of the civilized world is whether the patriot of this type must necessarily be either a "neuropath" or a "landless alien," as compared with him of the other sort; whether he be necessarily lacking in civic spirit, virility, and even soldierly virtues.

If the matter be of any concern, I gather that the author himself, so far from being physically a weakling, is a trained gymnast (of the type that our representatives will have to take into account at the next Olympic games) given to athletic exercises. He has also had sufficient medical training to have passed through a school of comparative anatomy. There are, therefore, no grounds for assuming offhand that he is of the nerveless type that faints at the first sight of blood; yet he writes of war with a shudder that the reader can feel in every line.

Yet—a contradiction his critics have not been slow to underline—this same man, who abhors the very thought of war, has written to the praise and glorification of war "like a professional panegyrist." While he was writing "The Human Slaughter-House," he was also engaged in etching some literary silhouettes, embodying the Dutch folk-songs, of the revolt of the Netherlands. The contrast is so striking that one or two of these "prose poems" may be worth quoting.

I

A reign of terror has dawned on the Netherlands. The Netherlands, ever proud of their freedom, are henceforward to be Spanish provinces. But the Netherlander has no mind for the honor. He cleaves obstinately to his chartered rights and to his nationality.

Then the Duke of Alva has come into the country in the Emperor's stead. He has brought in his train an army of Spanish soldiers, the gallows, and the executioner's axe. He has turned the country into a cemetery. A graveyard stillness reigns over it. For where three men foregather in the streets they smell out conspiracy in their midst. An ill-considered word, and the gallows, lowering in the background, silences the foolish mouth.

Setting their teeth, the Netherlander have to suffer it. The Spanish sword reaches the remotest village. Only in secret do they dare clench their fists. For the hangman's rack has a way of smoothing out clenched fists.

Terror lies on its chain like a wild beast. Only when it believes itself to be unobserved does it rise and sees the people lying on their knees, and hears a tortured country crying up to Heaven.

II

A star has risen against the sky of despair. The saviour of the Fatherland has been found. Egmont and Hoorn, the darlings of the people, have walked into the trap and have been beheaded in the market-place. But Orange has escaped. He has taken flight to Germany.

Orange, a clever brain! More clever than Spanish guile.

Orange, a brave heart! Braver than Spanish death and swords.

How calm was his countenance! How confident his speech! He is not the man to rush anything, to spoil anything. He will return in his own time.

They are already whispering it stealthily in one another's ear. The whisper is already passing from ear to ear, increasing to joyous certainty:

He is already in our midst. As yet he is in hiding. But on the morrow his call will ring out, and his confidence glow through every man's heart.

William of Orange!

III

The call has come. They are flocking in on every road. Groups of peasants and artisans. Masters, and apprentices among them. And the greybeards have taken their old weapons from the wall.

Halberds flash in the sunlight. Old-fashioned furniture of war. But still more ardently do their eyes flash. All are of one mind. All driven on irresistibly by one single impulse.

So they pass singing along the highroads. They had almost forgotten how to sing. But now it breaks out the more joyously in the sunlight—the solemn chant.

Dumfounded, the Spanish outpost, under cover of a hedge, gapes after them. Let them run, the spies. The spell is broken. Let them hear of it till their ears ring again.

The morning sun is shining. But we are marching to death and singing:

"Happy is he who knows how to die for God and his dear Fatherland."

IV

A pleasant farm hidden away in a garden. It is springtide. The garden is a blaze of white. Apple-trees in blossom. Beneath their boughs a man and a girl are standing close intertwined.

Beyond, on the other side of the hedge, they are passing along the village street. Their friends of the village. Their hour has come.

The girl's head is resting heavily on his breast, and her arm trembling round his neck. "Stay with me, only stay one day more. The wedding was to have been tomorrow. You will never come back! And we are so young—so very young. Look, how the blossom is falling. You, too, will lie on the ground like that, so dead and white. And I shall waste away and fade."

Then he looks into her eyes—sad unto death and fearful. "So you wish me to stay behind, and the others to go and die for us?"

She shakes her head without a word, and looks up at him with a smile amid her tears. Then he kisses her, and clasps her hand in farewell.

V

The groups have assembled. They have grown from day to day, and drawn nearer and nearer to the enemy.

And now the two armies are arrayed against each other—eye to eye. On the plain yonder you can see them—the Spanish troops flashing in steel—so close that you can distinguish their yellow faces in the sunlight.

What is their quest here on foreign soil? They are selling their blood for a hireling's wage, and turning themselves into hangmen to lay a free people in chains.

A distant glow is still glowering to the heavens. The last villages through which the Spanish dogs passed. They have left smoke and ruin behind them. Mangled corpses, the wailing of children. What do the strangers care? They have come into the country for loot.

There they stand, the destroyers! Splendidly harnessed, practised in war, and used to victory. Callously, as if at their handicraft, without much shouting, or much running about and movement, the array over there falls into line. A dangerous foe in its uncanny quiet.

Over against them the Netherlanders are a people assembled at haste. They are ignorant of drill, are ignorant how they ought to fight in ranks, and on horseback. But on the issue they are staking hearts filled with indomitable hate, filled full with undying love of country.

Beggars, the Spaniards once called them. And the Beggars are mindful of their nakedness. Their fists clench. Their teeth are set. And their lips are mumbling curses and hot prayers.

VI

It came to fighting. It came to murder. Death leaped up, and raced neighing across the battlefield, until it dripped blood—until at even, blinded with blood, it fled away into the darkness.

The battle is over now. The daylight is dying behind Bergen's towers. The shadows of night are blending with the shadow of Death.

It was a glorious fight. The wrath of a people is mightier than all the guile and strategy on earth.

But the victors are exhausted. Watch fires are ablaze. They all crowd round them to comfort themselves in their warmth.

Dark figures are whispering in groups. "Ha! How they ran! Whoever was overtaken was cut down—without mercy. They will remember the day. Will they come on again? How will the sinister Emperor take it? How far does his power reach? They will come on again. A bigger army! A bigger fleet!"

Look how the stars are gleaming. The air is clear. Even now you can see the heavens opening. And the Milky Way is glimmering down to meet you.

The sound of singing rises in the distance. An old hymn. A prayer of thanks of the days of our fathers. Those nearest by take it up. The chant leaps from fire to fire. The darkling field is singing. The night is singing. A choir raising their hands to Heaven, their voices to the stars.

Lord! Grant us freedom!

Where then lies the truth? In these "prose poems" aglow with martial enthusiasm, and ringing with the soldier's spirit, or in the relentless anatomical realism of "The Human Slaughter-House"? Or are both lies—"both deliberate conscious untruths, written under the inspiration of a social democratic lawyer?"

The explanation, as Lamszus see it, lies in the condition of the times. No one, he claims, could write of the revolt of the Dutch Republics otherwise than in the brave setting of flashing eyes, glittering steel, and the stirring clash of men-at-arms. But it is equally untrue to tell of modern warfare waged with picric acid and electric wires in the same spirit. The romance and glamour of warfare in the past are grinning lies when transferred to latter-day warfare, where long-drawn fronts of flesh and blood are opposed to machines of precision and the triumphs of the chemical laboratory. The anachronism becomes nothing less than the deliberate falsification of history. Dynamite and machine-guns, not the writer, have turned the "Field of Honor" into a "Human Slaughter-House," where regiments are wiped out by pressing an electric button.

In the hideousness of these scenes of future warfare the charge of exaggeration, of painting carnage red, is easy to raise, and difficult to rebut. Lamszus does not shirk it.

"What I have written was worked out empirically. It is a sum that is, mathematically, so incontestable that no one has hitherto ventured to dispute it. For the second factor in this sum is the albuminous substance of human brain and marrow. And when we hear that in the Russo-Japanese war thousands went mad, who would care to maintain that the nervous system of the civilized mid-European is hardier and tougher than that of Asiatics and semi-civilized Russians? 'The material has become softer,' says the authority of the staff-general. What now, when the sum total of acoustic and visual stimuli, of physical and psychic shocks, to which this 'softer material' is exposed, has, with every new invention, become more destructive in quality and quantity? To find the answer to such a simple problem did not assuredly call for a mathematical genius."

With the answer before us, the question rises whether it is more patriotic to blink it, to go on pretending that war is what it used to be—a soldier's death on the field of honor, or senseless automatic slaughter by machinery. It is against this latter mechanical aspect of war that the instinct of humanity, to which Lamszus has given voice in vivid words, revolts. Does it become a man better to look, with the full sense of his moral and ethical responsibility, the hideous fact in its face, or to continue to disguise it under a veil of romance woven round the pomp and circumstance of glorious war? In this sense "The Human Slaughter-House" of Lamszus' invention stands, as the Universal Peace Congress read it, for the revolt of the spirit of humanity, the spirit of progress and evolution, against the cumulative horror of the mechanics of modern warfare.

"For just as there is no room for the uncouth monsters of primeval times, for Mastodon and Brontosaurus, on the green earth today, so little will a nation of Krupp's steel plates be able to continue to live in the community of civilized nations."

None the less, a nation of men of virile breed will, he believes, be no less prompt to take up arms in defence of its heritage of culture than Prussia was in 1813, and to fight in its defence to the last gasp. For in the War of Liberation it was not drill, but the spirit of the people that saved the country.

"Thus the people in which we have belief will be irresistible in the council of nations, and be destined before every other to lead the nations to the work for which Nature has fashioned them.... Worthless indeed is the nation that would not stake its all for its honor. The only question that remains is what the spirit of this honor be; whether the appetite of savages and barbarians, hungry for spoils, impels me, or whether moral honor, the blood-stained desecrated face of God, inspires me."

With these bold words Lamszus concludes his apologia for the brutality of "The Human Slaughter-House."

OAKLEY WILLIAMS.

[Translation.]

To HERR LAMSZUS.

XIXme Congres Universel de la Paix a Geneve.

*Geneve,*1912.

DEAR SIR,

I have great pleasure in acquitting myself of the duty of expressing to you, in the name of "The Commission for Education, Instruction, etc.," composed of delegates of the most varied nations assembled at the World's Peace Congress, and, further, in the name of all Pacificists, our thanks for the distinguished word-picture of rare artistic originality and of gripping effectiveness of the wholesale murders of the future in "The Human Slaughter-House," *for having furnished the cause of peace with a weapon of considerable importance,* and for having more especially made a very valuable gift to the cause of every Pacificist.

May the blessing of its work be great!

On behalf of the Congress Commission for Education, Instruction, etc.

DR. A. WESTPHAL, *Secretary*.

CHAPTER I
MOBILIZATION

War! War is declared! So the news speeds hollow-eyed through the streets. We are at war. It's the real thing this time.

Mobilization!

The ominous word dominates the placards on the hoardings. The newspapers reproduce the proclamations in their heaviest type, and rumors and dispatches flutter like a ruffled dovecote round this day of Blood and Iron.

It is deadly earnest now. And this sense of the seriousness of it has numbed the State like a stroke of paralysis. But then a jar, as of a lever thrown over, goes through the vast iron fabric. And every one has got to yield to this jar. The time for anxiety and hesitation is over, for doubts and oscillation. The moment has now come when we cease to be citizens, from henceforward we are only soldiers—soldiers who have no time to think, who only have time to die.

So they come flocking in from the work-shops, from the factories, from behind the counters, from business offices, and the open country—they come flocking into the town, and every man falls in to stand by his native land.

"Four days from date" was the order on my summons. Well, the fourth morning has come, and I have said good-by to my wife and my two children. Thank God, the fourth morning has come, for the parting was not easy, and my heart aches when I think of them "at home."

"Where are you going, Daddy?" asked Baby, as I kissed her for the last time with my portmanteau in my hand.

"Daddy's going on a journey," said her mother, and looked at me with a smile amid her tears. "Yes, he's going on a journey, girlie, and you, little chap, you've got to be good, and do as Mummy tells you."

And then we got the parting over quickly, for Dora kept up her pluck until the last moment....

Now we are drawn up in the barrack-yard with bag and baggage—we of the rank and file—we reservists and militiamen, every man at his place by the table.

How serious their faces are. They reveal no trace of youthful high spirits or martial exuberance. Their expressions rather betoken deep thought.

"The war that in the end was bound to come"—so we heard and so we read in the papers. "That is bound to be so, that is a law of Nature. The nations are snatching the bread from one another's mouths; they are depriving each other of the air to breathe. That is a thing which in the end can only be settled by Force. And if it has to be, better it should be today than tomorrow."

We are mercenaries no longer—those hirelings for murder, who once sold their blood for money down to all and sundry. We are gladiators no longer—slaves who enact the drama of dying as an exciting spectacle for the entertainment of the rich, and for the lust of their eyes. It is to our native land we took our oath. And if it must be, we are resolved to die as citizens, to die in the full consciousness and full responsibility for our acts.

What will the next few days have in store for us?

Not one of us has probably ever, with his own eyes, seen a field of battle. But we have heard about it from others, and we have read in books of other men what a battlefield looked like in 1870-71, and, as though with our own eyes, we have watched the shells shattering human bodies. And another thing we know is that forty years ago in spite of inferior guns and rifles, over a hundred and twenty thousand dead stayed behind on the field of honor. What percentage of the living will modern warfare claim? Armies are being marshalled vaster than the world has ever seen. Germany alone can put six million soldiers in the field; France as many. Then the war of '70-'71 was nothing more than a long-drawn affair of outposts! My brain reels when I try to visualize these masses—starting to march against one another; I seem to choke for breath.

Then are we a breed of men other than our fathers?

Is the reason because we only have one life to lose? And do we cling so passionately to this life? Isn't our native land worth more than this scrap of life?

There probably won't be many among us who believe in the Resurrection, who believe that our mangled bodies will rise again in new splendor. Nor do we believe that our Father in Heaven will have pleasure in our murderous doings, that in that better world He will regard us other than as our brothers' murderers. But we bend our heads before iron Necessity.

The Fatherland has called us, and we, as loyal sons, obey the command there is no evading, submissively.... From today onward we belong to our native land, so the Major shouted a minute ago as he read out the articles of war.

And it's going to be the real thing this time.

The Sergeant-Major has already read the roll and checked it. We are already told off in fours. Now, in a long column, we are marching across the barrack-yard, for this very day we are ordered to doff our civilian dress, and don our new kit. This very day we have got to become soldiers.

Things are moving apace with us now.

CHAPTER II
SOLDIER

On the afternoon of the following day, the company is detailed for barrack drill. We are lying on our stomachs in the barrack-yard, and are being drilled in taking aim and firing lying down.

I have just been sighting.

In front of me on the barrack wall over there they have painted targets. Ring targets, head targets, chest targets. Three hundred yards. I take pointblank aim, and press the trigger. "Square in the chest." That ought to count as a bull's-eye.

Wonder how many clips of cartridges am I going to get through?

Wonder if there will be a bull's-eye among them?

If every man of those millions they are putting into the field against the enemy fires about a hundred cartridges, and there is one bull's-eye in every hundred, that works out at ... that amounts to ... and I can't help smiling at this neat sum in arithmetic ... then the answer is no one at all. That is a merry sum.

Snick!

The fifth cartridge tumbles out.

I ram in another clip of dummy cartridges.

How quickly and smoothly that's done. One—two seconds, and five cartridges are set in your magazine. Every one of them, if need be, can penetrate six men; it can penetrate palisades and trees; it can penetrate earthworks and stone walls. There is practically no cover left against this dainty little missile, against this little pointed cone.

And what a wonderful bit of mechanism this Mauser rifle is. How wretchedly badly off they were in 1870-71 with their rattletrap needle guns. A single feeble bullet at a time, and after you had fired it came the long, complicated business of reloading.

And yet the war accounted for well over a hundred thousand French and German dead.

I wonder how many dead this war will ac count for? If only every fifth man is left on the field, and if another fifth comes home invalided ... what will its harvest amount to then?

The whole of both countrysides are at this moment covered with soldiers lying flat, and all of them with their rifles at the ready, and all of them pointing the death-bearing barrels at one another, are perfecting themselves in the art of hitting the heart.

But behind them the guns are swinging up. The gunners are jumping down and dragging the trail round. They are already aligned, and a thousand black mouths are gaping uncannily toward the heavens.

We were once standing—we were in camp for musketry training at the time—and watching a battery firing with live ammunition. They had unlimbered and were ready to fire. The officers were peering into the distance through their field-glasses. The targets were not as yet in sight. We were all gazing intently toward the firing zone, where at any moment something might come into view.... There! Away over there. In the distance. Something is moving!

A shout of command.

The subaltern points to the moving target with his right hand. He shouts out the range. The gunners take aim, and:

"Ready! No. I gun. Fire!"

The missile is already a-wing, and for the space of a moment we feel the iron messenger flitting past. The air is a-hum. Boom—and a thousand yards in front of us the shell has exploded above the cavalry riding to the attack, and has spattered its rain of lead over the blue targets. And then Nos. 2, 3, 4, 5 and 6.

The next target was about a mile away, and the new range quickly found. Again the strange missile sped away and covered its measured course. It was a thing to marvel at, to see how it checked in the air of its own volition and burst. It seemed as though each one of these iron cylinders had a brain—as if it were endowed with life and consciousness—so certainly did it find its billet.

And when the battery had ceased firing and had limbered up, and the danger cone had been pulled down, we went out into the field of fire. There the linked targets under fire were lying. They had been struck down by the shrapnel—all, the whole line. Head, body, limbs;—we did not find a single figure there that had not been drilled through and through. We stood and marvelled at the accuracy of it, and with a silent shudder thought of targets other than contraptions of laths and canvas.

Wonder whether they have engines of such perfect precision on the other side?

How the experts have, day in, day out, been inventing and constructing new marvels of mechanism. The mechanical side of war has been raised to a high standard of genius and a fine art. Two hundred and forty bullets and more to the minute! What a marvel of mechanism one of those machine-guns is. You set it buzzing, and it spurts out bullets thicker than rain can fall. And the automaton licks its lips hungrily and sweeps from right to left. It is pointed on the middle of the body, and sprays the whole firing-line with one sweep. It is as though Death had scrapped his scythe for old iron; as if nowadays he had graduated as expert mechanic. They have ceased to mow corn by hand nowadays. By this time of day even the sheaves are gathered up by machinery. And so they will have to shovel our millions of bodies underground with burying machines.

Curse! I cannot get rid of this hideous; thought. It is always cropping up again. We have passed on from retail to wholesale methods of business. In place of the loom at which you sat working with your own hands, they have now set the great power-looms in motion. Once it was a knightly death, an honorable soldier's death; now it is death by machinery.

That is what is sticking in my gullet. We are being hustled from life to death by experts—by mechanicians. And just as they turn out buttons and pins by wholesale methods of production, so they are now turning out the crippled and the dead by machinery. Why do I, all of a sudden, begin to shudder? I feel as if it had suddenly become clear as daylight that this is madness—blood-red madness lowering for us there.

Curse! I must not go on brooding over it any longer, or it will drive me mad. Your rifle at the ready! The enemy is facing you! Has that ceased to be a case of man to man? What does it matter even if the bullet finds its billet more surely? Aim steadily—straight for the chest.... Who is it really facing me? The man I am now going to shoot dead! An enemy? What is an enemy?

And again I see myself on that glorious morning of my holidays, at a French railway station, and again I am gazing curiously out of the window. A foreign country and a stranger-people. The moment for departure has come. The station-master is just giving the signal. Then a little old woman extends her trembling hand to the window, and a fine young fellow in our carriage takes the wrinkled hand and strokes it, until the old woman's tears course down her motherly cheeks. Not a word does she speak. She only looks at her boy, and the lad gazes down on his mother. Then it flashes upon me like a revelation. Foreigners can shed tears. Why, that is just the same thing it is with us. They weep when they take leave of one another. They love one another and feel grief.... And as the train rolled out of the station, I kept on looking out of the window and seeing the old woman standing on the platform so desolately, and gazing after the train without stirring. I could not help thinking of my own mother. It was I myself who was saying good-by there, and on the platform yonder my poor old mother was in tears. Pocket-handkerchiefs were floating in the breeze. They were waving their hands, and I waved mine too; for I, too, was one who belonged to her....

And again I put my rifle to my shoulder, and take aim for the centre of the target.

I will not go on torturing myself with these thoughts.

The target seems to have been moved nearer to me.

Of a sudden it seems to me as if the blue-painted figure had stepped out of its white square. I gape at it. I distinctly see a face in front of me. I have got my finger on the trigger, and feel the tension of the pressure. Why don't I pull it through? My finger is trembling.... Now, now, I recognize the face. That is the young fellow at Nancy who was saying good-by to his mother....

Then the spring gives, and the great horror masters me, for I have fired straight into a living face. Murderer! Murderer! You have shot the only son of his mother dead. Thou art thy brother's murderer....

I take a hold on myself. I pull myself together. A murderer?

Folly! A spook!

You are a soldier.

Soldiers cease to be human beings. The Fatherland is at stake.

And without turning a hair I take aim at the enemy. If you miss him he will get you.

"Got him! In the middle of the chest."

CHAPTER III
OUR FATHER WHICH ART IN HEAVEN

We rejoined the Colors on Friday. On Monday we are to move out. Today, being Sunday, is full-dress Church Parade.

I slept badly last night, and am feeling uneasy and limp.

And now we are sitting close-packed in church.

The organ is playing a voluntary.

I am leaning back and straining my ears for the sounds in the dim twilight of the building. Childhood's days rise before my eyes again. I am watching a little solemn-faced boy sitting crouched in a corner and listening to the divine service. The priest is standing in front of the altar, and is intoning the Exhortation devoutly. The choir in the gallery is chanting the responses. The organ thunders out and floods through the building majestically. I am rapt in an ecstasy of sweet terror, for the Lord God is coming down upon us. He is standing before me and touching my body, so that I have to close my eyes in a terror of shuddering ecstasy....

That is long, long ago, and is all past and done with, as youth itself is past and done with....

Strange! After all these years of doubt and unbelief, at this moment of lucid consciousness, the atmosphere of devoutness, long since dead, possesses me, and thrills me so passionately that I can hardly resist it. This is the same heavy twilight—these are the same yearning angel voices—the same fearful sense of rapture——

I pull myself together, and sit bolt upright on the hard wooden pew.

In the main and the side aisles below, and in the galleries above, nothing but soldiers in uniform, and all, with level faces, turned toward the altar, toward that pale man in his long dignified black gown, toward that sonorous, unctuous mouth, from whose lips flows the name of God.

Look! He is now stretching forth his hands. We incline our heads. He is pronouncing the Benediction over us in a voice that echoes from the ~nb. He is blessing us in the name of God, the Merciful. He is blessing our rifles that they may not fail us; he is blessing the wire-drawn guns on their patent recoilless carriages; he is blessing every precious cartridge, lest a single bullet be wasted, lest any pass idly through the air; that each one may account for a hundred human beings, may shatter a hundred human beings simultaneously.

Father in Heaven! Thou art gazing down at us in such terrible silence. Dost Thou shudder at these sons of men? Thou poor and slight God! Thou couldst only rain Thy paltry pitch and sulphur on Sodom and Gomorrah. But we, Thy children, whom Thou hast created, we are going to exterminate them by high-pressure machinery, and butcher whole cities in factories. Here we stand, and while we stretch our hands to Thy Son in prayer, and cry Hosannah! we are hurling shells and shrapnel in the face of Thy Image, and shooting the Son of Man down from His Cross like a target at the rifle-butts.

And now the Holy Communion is being celebrated. The organ is playing mysteriously from afar off, and the flesh and blood of the Redeemer is mingling with our flesh and blood.

There He is hanging on the Cross above me, and gazing down upon me.

How pale these cheeks look! And these eyes are the eyes as of one dead! Who was this Christ Who is to aid us, and Whose blood we drink? What was it they once taught us at school? Didst Thou not love mankind? And didst Thou not die for the whole human race? Stretch out Thine arms toward me. There is something I would fain ask of Thee.... Ah! they have nailed Thy arms to the Cross, so that Thou canst not stretch out a finger toward us.

Shuddering, I fix my eyes on the corpse-like face and see that He has died long ago, that He is nothing more than wood, nothing other than a puppet. Christ, it is no longer Thee to whom we pray. Look there! Look there! It is he. The new patron saint of a Christian State! Look there! It is he, the great Djengis Khan. Of him we know that he swept through the history of the world with fire and sword, and piled up pyramids of skulls. Yes, that is he. Let us heap up mountains of human heads, and pile up heaps of human entrails. Great Djengis Khan! Thou, our patron saint! Do thou bless us! Pray to thy blood-drenched father seated above the skies of Asia, that he may sweep with us through the clouds; that he may strike down that accursed nation till it writhes in its blood, till it never can rise again. A red mist swims before my eyes. Of a sudden I see nothing but blood before me. The heavens have opened, and the red flood pours in through the windows. Blood wells up on the altar. The walls run blood from the ceiling to the floor, and—God the Father steps out of the blood. Every scale of his skin stands erect, his beard and hair drip blood. A giant of blood stands before me. He seats himself backward on the altar, and is laughing from thick, coarse lips—there sits the King of Dahomey and butchers his slaves. The black executioner raises his sword and whirls it above my head. Another moment and my head will roll down on the floor—another moment and the red jet will spurt from my neck ... Murderers, Murderers! None other than Murderers! Lord God in Heaven!

Then—

the creaking—

Light, air, the blue of heaven, burst in.

I draw a breath of relief. We have risen to our feet, and at length pass out of the twilight into the open air.

My knees are still trembling under me.

We fall into line, and in our hob-nailed boots tramp in step down the street toward the barracks. When I see my mates marching beside me in their matter-of-fact and stolid way, I feel ashamed, and call myself a wretched coward. What a weak-nerved, hysterical breed, that can no longer look at blood without fainting! You neurasthenic offspring of your sturdy peasant forbears, who shouted for joy when they went out to fight!

I pull myself together and throw my head back.

I never was a coward, and eye for eye I have always looked my man in the face, and will do so this time, too, happen what may.

CHAPTER IV
THE LAST NIGHT

I am lying in bed, and counting a hundred slowly. It must be close on midnight now, and I am still unable to get to sleep.

The room resounds to the noise of snoring. They are lying to the right and left of me, and if I turn over on my back, I am staring up at the wooden planking of a bed. For the cots extend all along the wall from door to window, one above the other, and in every cot a soldier is lying asleep.

Now and again one or other tosses about, and rolls heavily over to the other side.

Further away, near the window, some one is mumbling in his sleep. Suddenly he shouts out aloud: "And that wasn't me. I ain't touched a bit of the wire. D'you take me for a thief?"

It sounds exactly as if he were wide-awake. I am on the point of speaking to him. Then all is silence again, and I lie listening intently for what is going to happen next. But he keeps quiet, and goes on dreaming. He is still in the midst of his workshop; yet tomorrow he is going to be carted out to war.

And nothing but sleeping and snoring men all round me.

Wonder if any one else in barracks is lying wide-eyed and staring into the future?

My thoughts flit homeward. Wonder whether she slept well to-night? Wonder if she has chanced to be thinking of me? Wonder how the little chap is getting on? His teeth were giving him trouble.... It is not good to marry so young; the unmarried men who are called out now are better off. Wonder whether the war will last long? We have put by a little nest-egg. But what's the good of that in these times of famine prices? The allowance for wife and children is so small that it won't even cover rent. Where's she to turn for money when the post-office savings book is finished? She will have to go out sewing. But what's to happen when hundreds of thousands of others have to go out sewing too? Well, then she will have to start a little business, open a greengrocer's shop. But what's to happen when hundreds of thousands of others have to start a shop?

The State is taking charge of your wives and children, that's what it said in the regimental orders yesterday. Well, there is no use in imagining the very worst at the start. The war may be over quickly. Perhaps it will never get as far as big battles. Perhaps they will think better of it, and give way yet.

And then my mind feels at ease again. In spirit I see myself back again at my office-desk and writing invoices. A glance at the clock—it's close on the hour—only a few more strokes of the pen. So let's finish up quickly. Let's hang up our office coat on the nail and slip into another. And then get out into the street, for Dora must be waiting supper.

By this time we have already reached the bridge by the Town Hall, with the two big triple lamps.... Who is standing there by the railing of the bridge, and gazing down into the canal so motionlessly? It's a woman. She must have run straight out of the kitchen, for her apron-strings are hanging to the ground behind her anyhow. And all of a sudden her red-striped skirt strikes me as so familiar, and as I pass behind her she turns round without a word, and looks at me wild-eyed.

"Dora, is that you?"

Then she bows her face, streaming with tears, and says dully to herself:

"They have shot my husband dead."

"But, Dora," I shout to her anxiously—for it suddenly flashes upon me that she is ill—"why, here I am! Don't you know me any more?"

But she shakes her head, and turns away from me comfortless, and passes me by like a stranger.

"Dora!" I shout aloud, "Dora!" and stretch out my arms toward the vanishing figure. A sob chokes my throat...

Then I start, and am sitting up in bed, resting on my elbow. Through the window sounds the long-drawn reveille. Dawn is peeping through the panes.

So I did nod off after all, and I did not have a pleasant dream. But I have no time to be grumpy over it, for footsteps are ringing along the corridor. Hobnail boots clatter across the floor. The door is flung open.

"Turn out!" a cheery voice shouts in.

It is the sergeant on duty. By this time he has already reached the next door. And sleepy figures are rising from their cots, yawning and stretching their arms; are turning out and slipping, shivering with cold, into their clothes. Yawning, they stretch their limbs and flap their arms until the second more welcome morning signal, "Breakfast rations," lends life and animation to fasting men.

CHAPTER V
THE DEPARTURE

We are already drawn up in the barrack-yard in service kit. We have stacked our rifles and have fallen out. No one thinks of kit inspection or anything of that kind today. Everything is now being pushed on at racing pace.

"Fall in!"

"Stand by your packs!"

How heavy the full knapsack weighs in one's hands, and yet as soon as it is settled in the small of your back you do not notice it so very much.

"Stand by arms!"

"Slope arms!"

As if we were marching out for parade, the Captain's orders sound as crisp as that. We shoulder arms as smartly as if we were moving out on parade.

"Form sections! Right about turn! Quick march!"

And we swing round smartly in four at the command.

"Fifth, sixth, seventh, eighth company!" shouts the Major, who has pulled up in the middle of the yard.

We are the eighth company, and are following on the heels of the seventh. The gates of the barrack-yard are open. We are marching out. Our legs mark time on the pavement of the street in the goose-step of grand parade.

"March at ease!"

And the muscles of our legs relax and advance at more natural gait.

The streets are full of people. They are lining the pavement on both sides and watching us march past. Though it is still quite an early hour of the morning, yet the whole town is up and about. They weren't able to stay abed. They wanted to see the soldiers march out.

And they welcome us with their eyes and wave their hands to us.

A fifteen-year-old lad is running along beside us. His brother is marching in our file.

"Mother sends you her love; she says she is feeling better again—but she wasn't well enough to get up yet, else she'd have come with me this morning—but I was to give you this from her."

And the lad stretches his open hand out to his brother, and tries to hand him something wrapped up in paper—money! But the elder brother waves it aside.

"Put it away. Tell her I said she was to spend it on herself, and to look after herself properly, and be well and fit when we come back again."

Reluctantly the lad puts the money in his pocket.

A little ahead of us a young woman is tripping alongside. We have set a pretty smart pace, and she has to break into a run to keep up. But though her feet may stumble over the uneven pavement she never turns her eyes from her husband. What they may have to say to each other at the very last moment we can't catch. But we catch the expression of her face, and her comically touching devotion.

And now the crowds accompanying their soldiers through the streets become denser and denser. A few folk who are seeing members of their family off are running beside every section. White-haired fathers and mothers, with anxious looks, sisters, sweethearts, wives.

There is one among them of whom you can tell at a glance that she is about to become a mother. Well, she will be brought to bed lonely and desolate.

The man marching on my right, a taciturn yokel, who until now has been staring gloomily straight ahead of him, half turns to me.

"How many kids are there under way that'll never come to see their dads?"

And then he thaws, and begins to talk about his brother, who had to leave with the Army Service Corps two days before, and he was called on the Colors the very same day his wife was brought to bed, so that he had to leave her before she was out of the wood.

"Almost make you think us wasn't human beings."

The drums and fifes strike up briskly, and play a merry march.

Some one or other, somewhere in the crowd, sets up a loud, crowing sort of cheer.

"Hip! hip! hooray!"

And the others join in. It spreads all down the whole length of the street, and does not die down again. But it leaves my yokel unmoved.

"What's the good of that how-d'ye-do? Folks are fair crazed. There is no sense in it."

I glance at him out of the corner of my eye. He is impenetrably rapt in his own gloomy reflections. Then he begins again.

"Ah've left a wife and three kids to home. They're to get a few pence a day, the lot, and nought more. And that's what four people have got to live on."

Some one tries to cheer him up.

"Then some one else'll turn up who'll look after 'em!"

"What others?" comes the answer in a deep growl. "They'll have their hands full looking after theirselves. By the time I get home they'll have kicked the bucket, the whole lot of 'em. The best thing'd be never to come home no more."

Then the big drum breaks into his com-plaint. A dull reverberating throb. It is to usher in the regimental band, and orders the drums and the fifes to desist.

And then again, deep and monitory.

Boom!

The pipers begin to play the regimental march.

And now—the regimental band strikes up. You may kick against it as you will. The martial strain infects the excited streets, trumpets back from a wall of houses, stirs the blood so joyously, and exorcises the spectres of the night from your brain. Your muscles stiffen, you throw your head up, and your legs strut along proudly to keep step and time. And the rhythm of step and time infects the whole crowd. The effect on the crowd is electric. They are waving their hands from the pavements; they are waving their hands from the windows; they are waving their hands from the balconies. The air is white with pocket-handkerchiefs. And now some one in front begins to sing. They are shouting and singing against one another. The tune gains strength until it has fought its way through, and swirls above our heads like the wind before a storm.

The National Anthem!

The whole street is taking it up.

The regimental band has capitulated to the song that carries every one away with it. And then it solemnly joins in.

The crowds bare their heads. We can see nothing except glowing faces, figures marching under a spell, a nation afire and kindled to enthusiasm.

We march through the town singing ecstatically until we reach the station, until we at length come to a standstill on the platform reserved for us. The train is already standing there.

The bridge, beyond, leading over the rails is black with people shouting and waving down to us.

We are already told off.

Eight men to the compartment.

"Tara, tata!" The bugle calls us to entrain, and the doors are thrown open. We have scarcely stacked our packs and rifles, and donned our caps when the engine starts, and amid thunderous cheers we slide out of the station, and leave behind us a distant, fading roar, a dying hum—the town shouting her last farewell to her soldiers.

We make ourselves comfortable. We are sitting and smoking our pipes. Three, unable to change all at once, have already started a game of cards. Two more are sitting in the corner and putting their heads together. The yokel is by himself, and shows no interest in anything.

I am looking out of the window, watching the landscape fly past my eyes. The rejoicings are still hot in my blood. I have lived to see a great day. Wherever the bulk of the people rises above the dust of every day it becomes irresistible, and carries away with it even the man who would fain stand aloof, and keep his head cool.

And we hurry past forests and rivers, past meadows whose extent I cannot see, past hills that fade away into the blue of distance, past an immeasurably rich country that stands golden in its ears of corn.

And over it all shines the sun of one's native land.

And I would fain spread out my arms.

Yes, our native land is fair and great, and worthy that a man should shed his blood for it.

CHAPTER VI
LIKE THE PROMISE OF MAY

We have turned off the main road, and have to march over a field of stubble. A battle was fought here yesterday, for the field is sown with dead bodies. They have picked up the wounded. But as yet they have had no time to bury those who died where they fell.

The first dead man we saw struck us dumb. At first we hardly realized what it meant—this lifeless new uniform spread out there—from the way he was lying you could hardly believe he was really dead. It gave you a prickly feeling on the tongue. It seemed as if you were on manoeuvres, and the fellow lying there in a ditch had got a touch of the sun. A rough soldierly jest, a cheery shout was all that was wanted to raise him to his ramshackle legs.

"Hullo, you! Got a head? Keep a stiff neck."

But the words froze in our throat, for an icy breath was wafted to us from the dead man, and a chill hand clutched at our terror-stricken hearts.

So that was Death! We knew all about it now. That is what it looks like, and we turned our heads back and shuddered.

But then there came more and more of them.

And by this time we have become accustomed to them.

Strange! I gaze at these silent faces that seem to laugh at us, at these wounds that seem to mouth at us fantastically, as if they had I nothing to do with me. It strikes me all as so remote, so indifferent. As if all these dead bodies were lying in glass cases, as if I were in an anatomical museum, and were staring with dispassionately curious eyes at some scientific exhibits.

Sometimes no wounds at all are visible. The bullets have passed through the uniforms somewhere, and have gone clean through the softer parts of the bodies.

They have grown rigid in death in grotesque postures as if Death had been trying to pose figures here. There are certain schemes of Death that are always recurring. Hands out-stretched—fingers clawing the grass—fallen forward on to the face—that fellow over there lying on his back is holding his hand pressed tight against his abdomen, as if he were trying to staunch the wound.

In the country I was once watching them killing sheep. There a beast lay, and was waiting for the butcher, and as the short knife cut through its windpipe and jugular vein, and the blood leaped hot from its neck, I could see nothing but the big eye, how it enlarged in its head to a fearsome stare, until at last it turned to a dull glass.

All the bodies lying about here, as if bleating up to heaven, have got these glazed eyes, they are lying as if they were outstretched in the abattoir. Well, to be hit and to fall down dead, there's nothing to make a fuss about that! But to be shot through the chest, to be shot through the belly, to burn for hours in the fever of your wounds, to cool your mangled body in the wet grass, and to stare up into the pitiless blue heavens because your accursed eyes go on refusing to glaze over yet— —

I turn away from them. I force myself to look past these mocking, grotesque *posés plastiques* of Death.

And I am already spirited far away, and am sitting in my little study at home. My coffee cup is standing snugly to my hand. My book-case is beaming down on me. My well-loved books invite me, and in front of me my book of books, "Faust," lies open. And so I read, and feel the wonderful relaxation that comes after work stealing through my longing blood.

The door opens. A little girl, and a boy who has just learned the use of his legs, put their noses in at the door.

"Daddy, may we?"

I nod consent. Then they spread out their little arms, and rush at me.

"Daddy!"

They are climbing on to my knees now, and I give them a ride—"this is how we ride to war."

But they twine their soft arms round my neck until at length I put them down on the floor: "Now go to Mummy—"

And now— —

A new picture. How very plainly I see it. We have gone out of a Sunday afternoon beyond the suburbs, gone out with bag and baggage. I see the green fields bright and fair, and see the two kiddies bright and fair. They are rolling about in the grass and chasing the butterflies, and laughing up at me, and crowing with delight as they run after the ball I have thrown down for them to play with. And the sky stretches above us in its Sabbath blue, and so confidently as if it all could never come to an end. And Dora smiles at me with quiet eyes.

Then I come back with a start—I feel my knapsack chafing my back—I feel my rifle—I see the dead at my feet again—

My God! how can these things be? How can these two worlds be so terribly close to each other?...

And we pass on through this first spring crop of dead bodies. No one says a word. No one has a joke. How surreptitiously the others glance aside when some corpse, all too grotesquely mangled, meets their eyes.

I wonder what is passing through their brains?

Working men, tradesmen, artisans, and agricultural laborers, that's what they are for the most part. They themselves have as yet never smelled powder, nor ever been under fire. That, I suppose, is the reason why they have suddenly become so dumb.

Then a voice beside me says something abruptly, and it seems as if the voice rebounded hollow from the silence.

"The stuff is laying about here same as muck."

That was my yokel beside me. Then he, too, relapses into silence, and I feel as if I could read behind their shy eyes, as if all that is going on in these dull brains had suddenly become clear as daylight.

They're all drawn from that other world, where Life kissed us and cozened caressingly round our bodies. You have brought us up as human beings. That we have been human no longer counts. Life and love no longer count; flesh and blood no longer count; only gore and corpses count for anything now. How we used to tremble in that other world, when a naked human life was even in danger. How we rushed into the burning house to drive away the death for which some poor old paralyzed woman craved. How we plunged into the wintry river to snatch a starved beggar brat from the quiet waters. We would not even suffer a man to creep away out of Life by stealth while we looked on. We cut down suicides at their last sob, and hustled them back into life. Of our mercy we set up half-rotted wastrels with new bodies; with pills, elixirs and medicines, with herbalists, professors and surgeons, with cauteries, amputations and electrotherapy, we fanned the flickering life and fed the sunken flame with oxygen and radium and all the elements. There was nothing greater, nothing more sacred than Life. Life was everything to us, was for us the most precious possession on earth.

And here lies that most precious of possessions—here it is lying wasted and used up—spurned as the dust by the roadside—and we are marching along over it as over dust and stones.

CHAPTER VII
BLOOD AND IRON

The whole of that morning we had been marching in the eye of the sun without coming across a drop of water, for the country was not well watered, and there had been no rain for weeks. Our tongues were parched; our throats were burning. When about midday we passed through a farmyard, where we found a last remaining drop of dirty liquid, it seemed as if the water evaporated on the tongue before it ever reached our throats. Then we had been marched on interminably, so that it was almost with a sense of relief that we heard the first sound of the guns rolling up to meet us.

The firing grew hotter, and we soon left the main road and turned down a lane. We were pushed on at a smart pace. Our faces were glowing from thirst and heat. The column was enveloped in a thick cloud of dust. The taste of dust instead of water was on our tongues. The dust was lying thick as a layer of flour on our cheeks.

And we hurried on without a word. A quickset hedge barred the view on either side. Nothing but heavy footfalls, walking packs, black, clattering pannikins, rifles at the slope—hustle and dust.... Then some one blundered over a stone in his way, and looked as if he were going to fall into the back of the man in front of him ... but no shout of laughter greets it—we are pushing on almost at the double—at times, when a gap in the hedge slips past, we can catch glimpses of the line of skirmishers advancing over open country—now at length comes a check ... Halt! Order arms! ... and I am scrambling through a gap in the hedge on to the open fields ... open order at five paces distance.... The long-drawn line of skirmishers advances, rifles at the ready ... in front of us nothing but green fields in sight. In the heart of them gleams the crude yellow of a field of mustard. Ahead of us, just opposite our front, a dark wood ... not a trace of the enemy in sight. On our right they have already pushed on the advance line. On our left the skirmishers are just breaking through the hedge and opening out to extend our line of attack.

The heavy noise in the air is incessant.

I can't see where they are firing, and I can't see what they are firing at. The air is heavy with iron thunder. It closes like a ring round my chest. I am distinctly conscious that my chest is reverberating like a tense sounding-board——

What on earth is that?

A sound like the cracking of whips from somewhere or other ... the sound is so sharp, so distant, so intermittent, as if it were coming from the rifle-range....

Then—by my side a man falls down, falls on his rifle, and lies still, never stirs again ... shot through the head, clean through the brain ... that's what the cracking of whips means; it's coming from over there, out of the wood. Somewhere over there the enemy's sharpshooters are lying and lining its edge and opening fire on us.

What's the next thing?

Lie down—Mark distance—Cover!

But no order comes. We push on toward the wood undeterred, as if these bullets did not concern us in any way. The sharpshooters' fire is not hot enough as yet; we have not, so far, got into sufficiently close touch with the enemy.

It is an uncomfortable sensation to feel that over there muzzles are pointing straight at us. We are advancing almost as hurriedly and clumsily as 'rookies at their first field day.

As I move forward, I turn my head and look back. Behind me I sec new lines of skirmishers advancing one behind the other—supports to be pushed forward later.

What is that crawling along the ground behind our line?... there is one here, another over there—it looks so novel and so odd. They are crawling back out of the firing-line. And I see how one of them suddenly tries to rise, clutches his rifle with both hands, and hauls himself to his feet by his gun. And now he is spreading his arms out, tumbling over backwards, and flinging his hands away from him, far apart ... his hands are still flapping up and down on the grass. I am looking back as if fascinated while my legs keep on advancing.

But suddenly something begins to set up a rattle over there in the wood and buzzes like huge alarum-clocks running down.

"Lie down."

And there we are lying down, flat on our stomachs, as if we had already been mown down, for every man of us knows what that was. They have masked machine-guns in the wood over there; they are opening fire on us. I feel how my heart is thumping against my ribs. A machine-gun is equivalent to a company, the Old Man once explained to us, after we had been shot down in heaps to the last man by the machine-guns in the autumn manoeuvres.

What's the next thing?

Cautiously, without raising it, I turn my head. Behind us, too, the lines of skirmishers, close up to us, have disappeared from the face of the earth; they too, have gone to cover in the grass. Only outside the firing zone are they still being pushed forward.

Shall we have to retreat? Are we going to attack?

Then the order to fire rings out, and is zealously passed on from unit to unit.

"Rapid fire! Into the wood!"

Yes, but what are we to fire at? Lying down, there is nothing to be seen of the sharpshooters. They won't do us any harm; in another minute they will have disappeared among the trees. But the machines—they have hidden them away among the foliage to good purpose.

Our subaltern, lying a bare five paces away from me in the grass, raises himself on his elbows, and gazes intently through his field-glasses. I know what is vexing his soul. He is a handsome, splendid lad, for whom even we grizzled old-timers would go through fire and water, for he meets you as man to man, without sniffing or swagger, as it becomes a youngster. And the other day, when I was marching with the rear guard, we discussed Lilliencron's novels. Since then he has always appealed to me as if he had stepped straight out of one of these romances of war. He is all ablaze to glean his first laurels. But however much he may twiddle the focus of his glasses up and down and crane his neck, he cannot discover a trace of the enemy, and we blaze away foolishly at the wood, and may, for all I know, be bringing down leaves or birds from the trees there.

"Close to the big oak. To the right in the undergrowth," some one of the rank and file sings out.

I strain my eyes to the spot, and fail to see anything.

And again I hear the guns growling all round us. But somewhere out of the far distance a clear, long-drawn bugle-call rings out amid the iron bass. It thrills like nerve and brain against an iron wall.

Behind there, to the right—they are on the run there! And from afar the rifle fire rattles like mad.

"My men! Up with you! At the double!"

That came from our lot ... our subaltern is racing on with his drawn sword in his hand.... I am still prone, and have, almost automatically, drawn my right knee close up under my body ... they are rising to their feet to the left and right of me, and dashing on after him ... a wrench! and my knapsack slides lop-sided up the back of my neck ... then I jump up with my rifle in my right hand, and am running for all my legs are worth.

But as we rise to our feet the machine-guns in the woods begin to buzz, and to rain lead into our ranks, until right and left of me men yelp and drop twisted and tumbled to the ground.

"Down! Rapid fire!"

The line is prone and again we are blazing desperately into the wood, and can catch no glimpse of our enemy. Never a single arm raised against us, never the eye of a single man to challenge us. The wood, the green wood, is murdering us from afar, before a single human face comes in view.

And while to the right and left of me the rifle fire chatters incessantly, the grim mockery of it maddens my blood, and makes me see red before my eyes. I see scale-armor and visors ... high in their stirrups the knights burst blazing out of the wood, and I, a reckless horseman of the past, I leap into the saddle—my broad sword flashes clear and kisses the morning breeze—and now up and at them like a thunderbolt. Then eyes are flashing into mine and hands are raised for the *mêlée*—and stroke for stroke, breast to breast, the pride of youthful, virile strength.... Ha-ha-ha-ha! What has happened? Where have horse and rider vanished? Where is my sword? We are not even charging men. Machines are trained on us. Why, we are only charging machines. And the machine triumphs deep into our very flesh. And the machine is draining the life-blood from our veins, and lapping it up in bucketsful. Those who have been hit are already lying mown down in swathes behind us and are writhing on their wounds. And yet they are racing up behind us in their hundreds—young, healthy human flesh for the machines to butcher.

"Up! Get on! At the double!"

The gallant young subaltern dashes on ... he is waving his sword above his head recklessly ... a picture for a painter. I am rushing after him ... his cheer in my ears ... then the gallant vision begins to sway ... the sword flies from his grasp—the subaltern stumbles and falls face forward in the short, stiff stubble ... then I race past him ... I can hear nothing except the uncanny buzz coming out of the wood ... I literally feel how the lead is splashing into our ranks, how men are breaking down to the right and left of me.... "Down! Rapid fire!" ... I throw myself on my face, my rifle at the ready.... Why does the order fail to reach us? No shout comes from the subaltern, none from the non corns.... the nearest man a good twenty paces away ... and then one other ... only we three....

The first line is lying shot down in the stubble ... what's the next thing? The ground becomes alive behind us ... and clattering, panting and shouting ... and again the wood rumbles sullenly ... there they are, lying flat, breathing hard ... never a word ... rifle to the ready ... and shot after shot ... those are the sixth and seventh companies ... they have filled up our gaps.

"Up, up! At the double!"

The head is plunging on, the body after it, into the zone of bullets, and dashing forward with eyes fixed greedily on the ground to spy out the nearest molehill when we fling ourselves down. And when the excited "Down!" o'erleaps itself, we too tumble down as if we had been swept away. And look, it is advancing to meet us, that murderous wood.... "Up! At the double!" ... who can tell whether he has been hit or not?... behind there, out of the undergrowth—that's where it came from ... that's where the streak of bullets flashed ... there between the white larch trunks the beam of lead leaped out to meet us ... over there, behind that green wall, that's where Murder is sitting, and shooting our arms and legs away from our trunks. Slay her as she has slain us. Rend her to pieces, as she has rent us.

"Up! At the double!"

The body rages on in the whirl of the tempest—the wood, the wood!... the last muscle is still straining for the wood ... as if the soul had leaped free of the body, so the body chases after it—toward the wood ... lungs perforated by shot are running still; entrails riddled by bullets are still pressing on toward it ... and if you are not hit in the head, you are still jumping up once more; and if you fall, you are crawling on all fours—toward the wood....

What's happened?

Of a sudden a deep stillness falls....

The machines are silenced!

Not a single shot, not a single spurt of flame ... there—a rustling rising amid the undergrowth ... the branches overhead are swaying frantically against each other. Look! something is scurrying among the trees, and pushing and hauling—now, to crown it all, they are trying to save their precious machines from us.

Yah! yah! The earth reverberates dully and trembles under our tread ... a roar of cheers, clubbed rifles, that's how they are coming up behind us ... our reserves are driving the last assault home ... they are charging in dense mobs—sappers, sharpshooters, rifle-men ... a tall sapper jumps clean over me—I see how his eyes are flashing as he passes.... Up, after them ... there is the heather ... there is the entrenchment ... down with you into the trench and scramble up on hands and feet ... where are they? Where?—where?... there, by that belt of firs ... they will have disappeared in another minute—past thick, silvery tree-trunks, through the green beech leaves, with the sun laughing in them, the lust of blood charges red and naked ... headlong through the undergrowth—and now—there is something wriggling away so comically before our eyes, and twisting with sinuous dexterity in and out among the trees and the undergrowth ... there is something clinging to the machine as if it were ingrown into the iron.... Ha, ha!—in the clearing yonder the horses are waiting....

"Let go! Run for what you are worth—let go!"

But they won't let go ... for their horses are already ploughing through the undergrowth ... the wagon is straining to the traces ... in another minute they will have thrown their guns into the wagon ... and then so-long ... I am done—the trees are dancing round and round before my eyes ... I catch my foot in the root of a tree.... Lay on! Lay on! They are "ours" who have come up, and are laying on blindly on heads, and bayoneting bent backs and bared necks, till the whole tangle disperses squealing.... I drag myself to my feet. A lad, a mere boy, is sprawling over and clutching his abandoned gun ... with an oath some one dashes at him—it is my yokel bareheaded, his face distorted by rage ... the boy stretches out his mangled hand to ward him off, his lower jaw is waggling, but his mouth remains voiceless.... The next moment the fixed bayonet plunges into his chest ... first his right, then his shattered left hand seizes the blade as if in his death throes he were trying to pluck it out of his heart; so he clings tightly to the bayonet ... a thrust! a recovery!... a bright, leaping jet follows the steel ... and heart and breath gasp their last among the dead leaves....

All round men are lying slain on the brown carpet of the woods....

But the machines are still alive, and rage against the machines fires the blood, and consumes the flesh.... Up with the trenching tools!... with axes upraised they rush at the machines, and hail blows upon the barrels. The retorts wherein Death has brewed his potion shriek as though wounded ... the jackets burst ... the water flows out ... and the carriage leaps splintered into the air ... twisted metal, the spokes of wheels and cartridge-belts litter the ground all round, but we are battering and smashing everything underfoot until our hot blood has cooled its rage on the metal....

And now amid joyous cheers raise the thunderous shout of Victory. Let the pipes and the bugles ring out. This is Death on the stricken field! This is a soldier's frenzy and the joy of battle: to charge with bared breast against planted steel—to dash cheering with soft, uncased brain against a wall of steel. In such wholesale, callous, purposeful fashion vermin only are exterminated. We count for nothing more than vermin in this war.

And dazed and sick, we gaze at the machines, and the steel and iron littering the ground blink up at us full of guile.

CHAPTER VIII
THE SWAMP

For the whole of the forenoon we had heard firing in the distance, the thunder of cannon and the rattle of musketry. Our regiment had been marched hither and thither. The fight had drawn nearer and nearer. We were expecting to be under fire at any moment, and then we had to fall back again, and look for a new place to develop our attack. It seemed as if the orders that came through were contradictory, and this tension of uncertainty fell like a blight on our spirits, and got on the nerves both of officers and men. At length we had wound through a defile, the steep slopes of which, left and right, were thickly grown with trees. Things had got into a bit of a mess. We had had to force our way through undergrowth soaked with rain, through brambles and clumps of tall broom on which the green pods were still pendent. At times there was nothing in sight except the roof and wall of greenery.

We breathed more freely when at last the sky spread clear overhead again.

So now we have reached a green meadow, and are marching straight across it, but are still unable to see anything of the enemy's forces yet. Even the firing has died down, and has become more distant than before. It seemed as if we had come into another, remoter world, and—so we have; for soon we notice how soft the ground has become under our feet, how water is oozing up at every step. We shall, if we go on, be right in the middle of a swamp.

That is the reason of the solitude reigning all around us.

The terrain is impracticable.

To the right and left of us, and all about us, nothing but swamp, running out into a broad sheet of open water, the depths of which no one can guess, or tell whether it be fordable.

The head of the column is already swinging round and we are retracing our steps toward the defile to get out of the rat-trap.

And in the middle of the meadow:

"Halt! Form sections!"

The companies have fallen in. The officers have assembled, and are pow-wowing. We seem to have lost touch. The sergeant beside me is swearing up his sleeve, and is cursing at something about lunacy and blindman's buff. I am gazing up meditatively at the heights, overgrown with trees and undergrowth, and am thinking what fun it would be if we were to have to make our way back to the defile now, and in the thick of it the enemy were to break in on us right and left—no man would come out of it alive—the battle of the Teutoburger Forest recurs to me—I am trying to, make out if they are oaks or beeches over there——Of a sudden there is a flash of lightning from the undergrowth; the very firmament cracks and sways as if it were going to fall in on us....

"Lie down!" Horror screams somewhere or other.

And trembling, we lie down ... and over our heads rushes something that howls for our flesh.... What's the next thing? Up and at them now! Rush straight at the guns. Suffocate their fiery mouths with our flesh and bones.

"Up! Get up!"

The captain comes up to us at a run. The breath of the iron holds us tight pressed to the ground as if in a vice....

Turn your head away.

Now!

Now!

Then—A-a-h!

The vault of Heaven has cracked above us, and has spurted down on to the sand from above. Life is lying there, wriggling on the earth, and the hands that were clawing the ground are now clutching idly at the shattered air. I rise to my feet again.... I have not been hit. But the man who leaped up beside me—he is lying flat in the sand and screaming in a broken voice. He is lying as if he had been nailed firmly through his stomach to the earth, and as if he could not get free again. The body itself is dead, only the arms and legs are still alive. And arms and legs are working wildly through the air.

"Up! Get up! Quick march!" a voice yells in our ears. We no longer know who it is shouting to us, and we don't know from what quarter they have called us.... We leap to our feet. We leave the captain and the wounded in their blood; we start up and run away, and are running a race with the shells, for we are running for our bare, naked life. But the shells have the legs of us. They catch us up from behind in our backs, and wherever the invisible sheaf plunges hissing down, men are falling with it and rolling, helter-skelter in their blood. But we speed away over twitching and dismembered bodies, and over bodies turning somersaults, and look neither to the right nor to the left. We are on the run, and shrink into ourselves as we run. We draw our necks deep between our shoulders, for every man feels that the next moment his head will be leaping out from between his shoulder-blades from behind.

And eyes of iron are glaring at us from behind. The swamp! The swamp! The thought suddenly uprears its head in me. We are running blindly straight into the swamp. Only another twenty paces now—already the foremost have reached it, and, senseless in their terror, jump into it—the water spurts up high—and now—what has happened now? Their feet are stuck fast—they tilt over forwards—they claw for something to hold on to—the rifle flies out of their hand—and face forward they plunge into the water—and close on our heels they come stamping up—the tight-packed, maddened mob....

"Back! Get back!"

But every one has ceased to be conscious of what he is doing. And though our eyes start out of our head at the terror we see in front of us, Death is breathing its cold breath into the back of our neck.

And into the gurgling water, wriggling with bodies and alive with lungs, over human bodies writhing beneath the water, Death tramples us to the other bank. Any man who goes down is lost, for they are pressing on behind us past all holding. The water is already up to our armpits. But there is a firm bottom beneath our feet. True, the bottom may clutch at us, and cling round our feet. True, the water may bite savagely at our flesh with teeth and with nails. But whatever may be trying to draw us down to itself from below, we trample underfoot. The shoulders of a form emerge; they plunge down again, and disappear. The faces of drowning men emerge and cleave to the light, and sink gurgling into the depths. Lost arms wave about in the air and try to find support on the surface of the water. We dodge these arms, for whomever they may seize they draw down with them to Death.

And in the thick of this hurly-burly of Death, amid these whistling lungs, amid these panting, red, panic-stricken faces, the cloud of shells strikes home, and hurls its hail of iron overhead. The water spurts up in jets.

And again!

Explosions and screams, and the hissing of lead, and the shrieks of men, and blood and water foam up, till no one knows whether he has been hit or is still alive; for in front of me—so close that I could clutch it—I see a jugular vein, ripped through, spurting in an arch like a fountain—and in his blood the fellow hit staggers back, and blood and howls surfeit the black flood, until it is at length reddened with human blood—Get on! get on! Don't look round! There—the other bank over there! There Life is standing and spreading out his arms toward us. Get on! Before they have murdered all of us in this swamp! Get up! Get up! Thank God! The water's falling! Only up to the hips now—only up to the knees.

And now——

Our feet leap on to the dry, blessed land and strike forward beyond all control, and race over the field. They refuse to obey any orders. They are racing—racing toward the protection of the forest beckoning us of its mercy.

There! Headlong in among the trees, and into the bushes, into the thorns. There they are falling lifeless to the ground, their faces buried in the soil, and they are squeezing their eyes tight, to shut out the sight of the accursed blue of heaven that spat down on us so treacherously—You dogs! You beasts! To shoot us down from behind—it is nothing more nor less than cowardly assassination.

And slowly breath and consciousness return to us again, and when we have come to our senses we look at one another with dumb eyes, and these eyes presage nought that is good.

A great, unspeakable Horror that will never be allayed again has risen in these eyes.

CHAPTER IX
THE WHIRLING EARTH

Half-way on the march some one fell down beside me, flung out his arms, clawed himself tightly to the earth, and screamed and gasped against the soil. Barely half an hour later we saw another who had fallen into convulsions. And when we were lying in a damp ditch waiting for the enemy, a man suddenly jumped up, and shrieked, and ran away. He laughed back at us from afar until he vanished from our sight in the rain. The shrieking and running away had infected us all. 'Twon't be long before it will be your turn.

One night when we were lying in our trenches, and had fallen asleep to the thunder of the guns, I suddenly started up—confused—dazed; and lo, the stars were standing bright in the dark, rainless sky, and shone down solemnly, ah God! how solemnly, on the turmoil, as if nothing in this world mattered. Yet there—in front of me, before my very eyes —glimmered a red reflection—that surely must be a pool of blood, for the stars are mirrored in it so redly—and suddenly a blind rage overtook me to howl aloud and clench my fists, and to scream in the very face of the great Master up above there—But I had neither time to howl nor to run. For in this self-same night it so happened that an uncanny whirr fell on our ears from out the distance. That was Death flying toward us on propellers. The spectres of the night whirred above us; we shot blindly into the air—for every moment the storm was bound to break over us.... Torpedo tubes above us ... they'll spurt in a minute ... they're going to fling down dynamite ... and then the magnesium bombs blazed out ... cries and crashes rose wherever we looked ... then they are gone again ... but we had to retire from our trenches ... senselessly, like automata, we marched for the whole of that day. I felt the goose-flesh creeping over my skin; my nerves ached, and if the bayonet were not at the small of my back I should chuck my rifle away, and roll sprawling in the damp sand.

And yet four days afterward they have contrived to get us to make a stand again. For in our rear, on the other bank of the river, our regiments have crossed, and are groping for new positions. But we have to cover their passage at any cost.

We were now drawing on our last reserve. We were still standing with our spades in our hands, and throwing, with aching backs and arms, more soil on the works, when in front of us we saw figures passing up and down on the grey, twilight field. They were grubbing the soil up busily, and were putting something we could not see into holes, and covering it in again. They went about their work noiselessly—no incautious step and no unguarded movement—and when they came back again and passed us, and marched on, their faces were livid and their lips dumb. They proved themselves to be first-class moles. They had done a good bit of work. They had undermined the earth. They had stuffed the ground with explosives, and if the enemy comes to-night we shall repay the gifts they lavished upon us from the sky the other day with interest. They have arranged it all like a rat-trap.

Over there, beyond the mined field even, two companies are lying in extended order. And midway between them, without a vestige of cover, stands our battery on the open field. It is planted there as if it were doomed to be delivered into the enemy's hands.

And now we are lying in our long trenches, and are peering out into the field, with our eyes glued to the sharply outlined silhouettes of the guns. The sun has set some time ago.

From the far distance the thin rattle of musketry reaches us clearly.

Wonder if it'll last much longer?

Our orders are to remain under arms.

We have put on our overcoats. The night is chilly, and lowering, I gaze out over the field of death—nothing makes any difference to me now—if only it were over quickly.

A scout has come in, and delivers his report in a whisper.

Our instructions are not to fire before the order to fire is given, and—then to fire into the air.

In the background, far on the horizon, the ground rises, and the gray skyline stands out against the cloudy sky. The musketry fire has become hotter from minute to minute, and has increased to a threatening rattle. To the right and left of us fighting is in full swing. In front of us the mined field lies silent, and the two companies too, are lying silent in their rifle-pits.

I am conscious that I am terribly tired—I can no longer keep myself on my feet—my head sinks down on my rifle—my eyes close—but the overstrained nerves are still alert.

And now——

The earth reverberates sullenly.

That's our battery! It is firing straight into the darkness. So our turn is coming now.

We hear how "ours" over there are opening fire, and how it suddenly increases, and dies down, and then again swells to a maddening rattle. That is an attack by sharpshooters in overwhelming strength ... they cannot be very far from one another now ... and yet the battery goes on bellowing, and luring the enemy to assault....

And now a martial symphony rises over the dark country ... bugles shrill through the darkness, and drums are rolling sullenly ... that means a general assault ... there rises a sound of shouting and tramping ... a thunderous roar of triumph rises to the dark sky ... that is the shout of victory from a thousand throats ... in their thousands they have charged "ours" over there, and have crushed them by assault.... Ha, ha! they have taken a battery by storm....

Why, of a sudden, has silence fallen ... what is the object of it ... now it's our turn....

"Into the air! Rapid fire!" And the volley, crashes. And look there ... over there the cheer rings out again ... the signals for assault sound, and thousands of voices are shouting it simultaneously ... there they are foaming up ... they are charging on, drunk with victory, in closed ranks ... they are rolling with a roar over the mined field ... they are trampling the earth, as if with horses' hoofs ... that means Death ... I am lying rigid ... now it must break, now ... I open my mouth wide ... my rifle is trembling in my grasp....

And then—

The Earth has opened her mouth ... lightnings, crashes and thunderings, and the Heaven splits in twain and falls down in flame—the earth whirls upwards in shreds ... men and the earth blaze and hurtle through the air like Catharine wheels ... and then ... a crash, a maddening uproar, strikes us full in the chest, so that we reel backward to the ground, and half-consciously struggle for breath in the sand ... and now ... the storm is over ... the pressure of the atmosphere relaxes off our chest ... we breathe deep ... only scattered, dancing flames now and squibs ... fireworks....

But what on earth has happened?——

We peer out fearfully over our earthworks.

Has red Hell opened its mouth:

There rises a noise of screams and yells, an uproar so unnaturally wild and unrestrained that we cringe up closer to one another ... and, trembling, we see that our faces, our uniforms, have red, wet stains, and distinctly recognize shreds of flesh on the cloth. And among our feet something is lying that was not lying there before—it gleams white from the dark sand and uncurls ... a strange dismembered hand ... and there ... and there ... fragments of flesh with the uniform still adhering to them—then we realize it, and horror overwhelms us.

Outside there are lying arms, legs, heads, trunks ... they are howling into the night; the whole regiment is lying mangled on the ground there, a lump of humanity crying to Heaven....

Clouds are arising from the earth ... they are rising crying aloud in the air ... they pass over us in thick drifts, so that we can see the wounds steaming, and can taste blood and bones upon our tongues....

And then a spectral vision rises before my eyes ... I see red Death standing outside there on the plain ... the clouds reveal a face grinning down on the symphony ... and suddenly a clear note detaches itself from the darkness—a tune which enraptured Death is playing to himself till his fiddle splits ... is that a human being coming up, running, here?... he is coming with a rush ... he will leap upon our backs ... halt! halt! halt! He stumbles upright into the trenches, and tumbles sobbing and howling, among our rifles. He strikes out at us with hands and feet ... he is crying and struggling like a child, and yet no man dares go up to him ... for now he is rising on his knee ... and then we see! Half his face has been torn away ... one eye gone ... the twitching muscle of the cheek is hanging down ... he is kneeling, and opening and closing his hands, and is howling to us for mercy.

We gaze at him horror-stricken and are paralyzed ... then at length the yokel—and our eyes thank him for it—raises the butt of his rifle and places the muzzle against the sound temple ... bang!... and the maimed wreckage falls over backward and lies still in his blood....

And again the darkness casts up shapes ... they run up and reel about like drunken men ... they fall over and pick themselves up anew ... they race forward through the night in zigzags, until they at last collapse exhausted, and lie still under our very eyes and make an end of it....

And at length some one comes crawling toward us ... he is crawling up on all fours ... he is dragging something behind him with his body, and all the time he is whining like a sick dog, and is howling shrilly in long-drawn tones ... he is still crawling along I fast—and when he has reached us we see—I and the blood stands still in our hearts—they are his entrails hanging out of his body ... his belly has been ripped up from below ... he is crawling, he is crawling up on his entrails ... he is coming ... the entrails are coming ...

horror breaks out from every pore ... for hardly three paces away from me he lies still ... and then ... May God forgive me!... he raises himself slowly on his hands ... he succeeds for a moment ... and looks ... Merciful God!... he looks at me, and refuses to let my eyes go again ... I can see nothing except these great, death-stricken eyes.... Merciful God! ... his eyes, those eyes! Those are a mother's eyes looking down on me unspeakably ... that is a son of his mother lying there before us butchered.... I will break out of my fastness.... I will throw myself on him, sobbing, and kiss his face, and bathe his anguish away in my tears.... I will do it! I will! ... and cannot stir myself from my rigid tension.... Then the monstrous strain relaxes—his arms give way ... he falls forward on his face and sinks down on his tortured body. His hands twitch once more ... then he lies still and kisses Mother Earth, who has slain her children so horribly....

I am done ... my hands are trembling.... Then all of a sudden, a voice behind us begins to sing ... solemnly—long-drawn.... "Now thank we all our God" ... that is Madness singing there ... we are all next door to madness.... I look round, and see gray, distorted faces, and blazing, startled eye-balls.... And suddenly the singing voice changes to a loud, impudent burst of laughter....

"Ha! Ha! Ha! Ha!" The laugh is full of horror, and mingles with the dying whine beyond.... The laugh grows ever louder, and ever wilder, and laughs in triumph at the naked, pitiful dying, littering the ground.

"Drummers! Strike up!" shouts the voice.

"Uncover for prayer!"

We recognize him; he is a reservist belonging to some pious sect. A sergeant has seized him, and tries to hold him ... the captain has run up, but the madman tears himself away and runs ahead of them to a rifle-pit ... he stands aloft, a black, wild silhouette against the pale sky, and spreads out his arms in blessing over the sick night ... he stands there like a rapt priest, and raves, and is blessing the mangled darkness. "In the name of the Father, and of the Son, and of the Holy Ghost."

Then arms seize him from behind and pull him down ... they drag him to the ground.... "Our Father" he howls aloud, and strikes and kicks out all round him, and goes on praying from his raging body until at length breath fails him ... they have tied him hand and foot, and have gagged him....

But now the Thing-that-Couldn't happens—that none the less was bound to happen.

And when the voice calls out it comes over me as if I had lived it all once before....

"Captain!" shouts the hard, naked, impudent voice we all know. "Haven't you got any cotton wool for us to plug our ears with?"

We have all turned round as if at the word of command. It is the militia-man, the yokel, standing facing the captain and gesticulating at him. "I only wanted to ask if those are wild beasts, or if they're what are called human beings you've torn to pieces there?"

But curt and sharp, as we knew it, the rasping note of command responds:

"What the devil's the matter with you? Pull yourself together. Can't you hear? Get back to your place at once."

But then it bursts out, the voice of Nature, and resounds so harshly, and tears down all barriers.

"Murderers!" roars a blasphemous mouth. "Murderers of men! We shall have to knock them all on the head like dogs."

We all start as if under an electric shock ... that was what was on the tip of the tongues of all of us ... that was the climax that was bound to come ... we cannot endure to go on lying in this charnel-house any longer....

"You mind what you're about." The other's wrath breaks out once more ... and then we know it for certain, the captain is a fool ... he has lost the game from the very start ... and now ... it is like a shadow play before my eyes ... like a ghostly kinematograph.... I see that the militia-man has drawn his bayonet ... the captain is standing facing him with his revolver in his hand, and gives him an order ... he promptly gets a blow with the butt end of the rifle on his head that fells him to the ground without a sound ... and they leap up from all the trenches.... "Murderers!" they cry. "Murderers! Kill them!"

There is no stopping it now.... I feel I have gone mad.... I do not know where I am.... I see wild beasts all round me distorted unnaturally in a life-and-death grapple ... with bloodshot eyes, with foaming, gnashing mouths, they attack and kill one another, and try to mangle one another.... I leap to my feet.... I must get away, to escape from myself, or in another minute I shall be in the thick of this maddened, death-doomed mob.... I stumble over the rifle-pits.... I race out into the night, and tread on quaking flesh ... step on hard heads, and stumble over weapons and helmets ... something is clutching at my feet like hands, so that I race away like a hunted deer with the hounds at its heels ... and ever more bodies—breathless—out of one field into another.... Horror is crooning over my head ... horror is crooning beneath my feet ... and nothing but dying, mangled flesh....

Has the whole earth exploded then?... Are there nothing but dead abroad this night?... Has every human being been fusilladed?

How long have I been running?... I hear how my lungs are whistling ... and hear how my temples are beating ... my breath is choked.... I am done.... I stagger backwards ... am falling dead to the ground ... no! I am sinking back on something soft, and sit still motionless, and listen intently to the night.... I can hear nothing except the blood in my ears ... all of a sudden there is a light in my eyes like bright, clean daylight ... the sun is shining ... then I realize it, it is my own head ... visions are teeming in my brain, and are teeming out of my head, one unwearyingly on the heels of the other.... I see the regiments marching out ... they are passing by in the bright sunshine ... the Blues from over there, the Reds from over here; they are marching against each other in long array.... Now they halt, and are standing drawn up against each other on a huge front ... ready for the fray ... then our captain's voice on this side rings out.... "Ready?" ... and the rifles on both sides are raised. I see the black mass of the muzzles ... they are scarcely ten paces apart ... they are aiming straight for the chest.... "Stop!" I am trying to cry out, "Stop! You ought to attack in open order with seven paces intervals." ...

Then our captain's voice rings out again, "Fire!" ... the volley crashes, and behold! not a man is hit ... they all are standing there unscathed ... they have fired into the air ... and with shouts of joy the ranks dissolve ... they rush toward one another ... the rifles fall to the ground ... but they rush into one another's arms, and fondle one another, and laugh aloud as children laugh ... then they fall back into line ... they shoulder their rifles ... right about turn!... the bands strike up a joyous march, they march off with bands playing—every regiment to its own home....

And now I catch myself singing an accompaniment to it aloud.... I am beating time with my right hand, and supporting myself on my seat with my left ... and something trickles oddly across my hand—something like warm water.... I raise my hand to my eyes ... it is red and moist ... blood is flowing over my white hand ... then I realize it, the white thing under me is not a heap of sand.... I have been sitting on a corpse ... horror-stricken, I rush about ... and one is lying over there, too ... and there, and there!... Merciful God! I see it plainly now; there are only dead to-night ... the human race died out this very night ... I am the last survivor ... the fields are dead—the woods dead—the villages dead—the cities dead—the Earth is dead—the Earth was butchered to-night, and I, only I have escaped the slaughter-house.

And it comes over me as a great thing, a pathetically great thing—now I know what my destiny is—lowering, I watch my own actions, and wait to see how I shall accomplish it—I mark how I am slowly putting my hand into my pocket—before I left home I took my pocket-pistol with me. I am holding the toy in my hand—the steel is looking up at me and blinking at me—I am gazing with a smile into its black, confiding muzzle—I am holding it against my temples—I pull the trigger, and fall over backward—the last of mankind on this dead earth!

EPILOGUE WE POOR DEAD

They have now covered up our hot breath with earth. Why are you blinking at me with your bleared eyes, my brother? Are you not glad? Don't they envy us our sweet death? They have laid us out in a picturesque row, and you need only turn your head to rub against human flesh at once, and if you turn your yellow eyeball, you can see nothing but corpses in the twilight. One beside the other, that is how they are sleeping. And corpse upon corpse, ever more of them, through the whole length of the loose soil of the potato-field, and we even fill the whole adjoining field of roots.

Wonder whether the sun still goes on shining above us?—whether they still know how to laugh in the towns as we used to in our time? Wonder whether my wife still goes on remembering her dead husband—and my two kiddies—whether they have already forgotten their father? They were so tiny at the time—another man'll come along—they will call another fellow father—and my wife is still so young and fair.

We poor dead heroes! So do not disturb our last sleep any longer. We had to die to enable the others to live. We died for our native land in its straits. We are victorious now, and have won land and fame, land enough for millions of our brothers. Our wives have land, our children, our mothers, our fathers have land. And now our poor native land has air to breathe. It need no longer be stifled. They have cleared the air of us. They have got rid of us, of us who were far too many. We are no longer eating the bread away from other folks' mouths. We are so full-fed, so full-fed and quiet. But they have got land! Fertile land! And ore! Iron mines! Gold! Spices! And Bread!

Come, brother philosopher, let us turn our faces to the earth. Let us sleep upon our laurels, and let us dream of nothing but our Country's Future.